BECOMING A HEALTHY TEAM

Workbook & Exercises

BECOMING A HEALTHY TEAM

Workbook & Exercises

Stephen A. Macchia
With Justin Schell

LEADERSHIP
TRANSFORMATIONS INC.
FORMATION | DISCERNMENT | RENEWAL

Published by Leadership Transformations
PO Box 338
Lexington, MA 02420
www.leadershiptransformations.org

Printed in the United States of America

Library of Congress Cataloging-in-Publication Data
Macchia, Stephen A., 1956-

    Becoming a healthy team : workbook & exercises / Stephen A. Macchia.

       p.   cm.

    Includes bibliographical references.

    ISBN 978-0692368756 (pbk.)

    1. Group ministry 2. Teams in the workplace. 3. Sports teams. 4. Christian leadership. 5. Leadership—Religious aspects—Christianity. I. Title.
BV675.M27 2005
253p.7—dc222005014387

*Dedicated to all teams
who are searching for
deeper unity with God and
one another*

CONTENTS

PREFACE

When Justin Schell suggested writing Exercises for *Becoming a Healthy Team* I was immediately delighted with the idea. It's one thing to read and ponder the principles of team health contained in *Becoming a Healthy Team*, and another altogether to practice those same principles with the men and women you've been called to serve as a team.

What you have before you is a plethora of ideas to consider trying with your team. There's plenty to choose from whether you wish to take each major principle one-at-a-time, or to randomly select exercises according to the current needs of your team. Whichever way you choose, your experiences will significantly impact the quality of your team life ... that's for sure!

It's hard work both leading and participating in a healthy team. Many aspire to this goal, but not everyone achieves it. We know from history and experience that to become a healthy team requires practice. So, why not make it fun and engaging for all?

The way that Justin has organized this material will make it easy to use. He's kept the overall outline of the book, *Becoming a Healthy Team*, all the while adding creative ideas to consider every step of the way. From Bible studies, to reflection, fun ideas, retreats, and even times for confession and discipline ... each one keeping the leader and team focused on the singular goal of team vitality.

I'm thrilled to commend this fine resource to you and your team. Try out the exercises and let us know how they helped forge stronger allegiances among your team members. We'll celebrate with you and continue to encourage you through the additional ministry resources of Leadership Transformations at www.LeadershipTransformations.org. Visit us today and sign up for our free monthly spiritual formation resource, *Silencio*.

God bless you and your team with the abundance of his mercy, joy and peace.

For the health of ministry teams everywhere,

Steve Macchia
Founder and President, Leadership Transformations
Author, *Becoming a Healthy Team*

INTRODUCTION

"The crux of the matter is that teams are a lot of work."[1] Anyone who has been a part of a team for very long would most likely give a hearty "amen" to this honest statement. The multitudes of church splits that have come due to staff and/or ministry team conflict have been widely documented. It has long been the case on the mission field that the number one reason for missionary attrition is the inability of missionaries to get along with one another. Still other teams are emotionally and relationally healthy, but desire to go even deeper with one another in their shared faith in Christ and their shared ministry, but they often have no idea of where to begin.

In *Becoming a Healthy Team*, you will get a strong foundation of what it means to be a healthy ministry team. You will hear from God's Word the Lord's expectations for a ministry team, and find that the rich community that God calls for goes back to the Trinity itself where Father, Son, and Spirit form the perfect team working together "from time past throughout all eternity" in perfect love, trust, and cooperation. You will even receive some of the best thoughts on leadership distilled and presented in very practical ways.

The material presented in *Becoming a Healthy Team* is the foundation on which our present study is built. Our goal is not to give you more information about teams, but to get your team interacting with one another over the material found in Becoming a Healthy Team. We will do this through designed activities that correspond with the five traits and twenty sub-traits of vital leadership which can be found on the following page. In general, these activities are designed to get your team communicating. There are other types of activities (ropes courses, etc.) that ask your team to adventure together, and these can be very beneficial; however, for most teams, the need of the hour is direction in simply conversing with one another over important team issues. These activities will come in all shapes and sizes, from Bible studies, to directed conversations, and even community shared spiritual disciplines. Some of these activities will be very easy while others will stretch you to the point of breaking. For each trait and sub-trait there are multiple exercises that a team can do to nurture these vital areas of team life, so what follows will be only the beginning of the journey for your team.

---

1.   Stephen Macchia, Becoming a Healthy Team, (Leadership Transformations, 2013), 18.

TRAITS OF VITAL LEADERSHIP

A Christian ministry team is a manageable group of diversely gifted people who hold one another accountable to serve joyfully together for the glory of God by:

- Sharing a common mission
- Embodying the loving message of Christ
- Accomplishing a meaningful ministry
- Anticipating transformative results

Healthy Teams TRUST
- Build Trust through Community
- Build Trust through Celebration
- Build Trust through Communication
- Build Trust through Conflict

Healthy Teams EMPOWER
- Empower through Gifts and Passions
- Empower through Defined Responsibilities
- Empower through Teachability and Resourcing
- Empower through Delegation and Accountability

Healthy Teams ASSIMILATE
- Assimilate through Cross-Pollination
- Assimilate through Others-Orientation
- Assimilate through Systemic Direction
- Assimilate through Ministry Multiplication

Healthy Teams MANAGE
- Manage through Strategic Plans
- Manage through SMART Goals
- Manage through Systematic Administration
- Manage through Results Evaluation

Healthy Teams SERVE
- Serve through Heartfelt Prayer
- Serve through Discernment of Need
- Serve through Fulfillment of Call
- Serve through Transformation of Life

TEAM ACTIVITIES & EXERCISES

You will find the following activities and exercises peppered throughout the workbook. Each one will help propel you on your way to team vitality. Watch for the activities and exercises marked with section headers below to alert you to an opportunity to engage in a shared practice. It is important to incorporate a wide range of activities because not all team members are the same, and thus, need to be challenged in a variety of different ways. The following is a brief introduction to those sign-posts.

| BIBLE STUDY |

Give as much time as you desire to digging into the suggested passages. There will be guiding questions provided, but do not allow that to hinder you from spending more time understanding what God might be saying to you through His Word.

| SHARE |

These are opportunities to get to know one another through the sharing of life experiences. Often it will require very surface level information, but vulnerability is encouraged when the situation is appropriate. A mentor once said to me, "If I don't know who you are, how can I love you?" What a great question for every team and team member.

| REFLECTION |

Sometimes the thoughts of others can be a great challenge to us. As you read the reflections of others, give yourself and your team time to reflect on what is read and how what is read might be touching a place in the heart of some on the team which needs to be shared.

| CONFESSION |

We can all agree that eventually everyone on the team will have a bad day, say something that they regret, or derail the team's mission in some regard. We do not wish to give the devil a foothold, and these activities will help to foster the keeping of short accounts with one another.

| DISCIPLINE |

It is our relationship with God that links us together as a ministry team. These links represent that truth. Similarly, disciplines that may not seem spiritual, when undertaken together, can produce a greater unity and synergy. Committing to a discipline as a team can not only foster our relationship with God, but bring us closer to one another as well.

| ACTIVATE |

Sometimes action is required to pursue deeper community. These activities may require planning, thought, and execution, but your team will feel the benefit and appreciate the effort it takes to accomplish these exercises.

| FUN |

One of the best ways to get to know someone is to laugh with them and to make them laugh. These light hearted activities might require some bravery to enter into a time of planned silliness, but they hopefully will allow for your team to relax and enjoy each other.

| RETREAT |

Get away and get with God together. Allow some sacred time and space to be created for the sake of discovering, remembering, embracing, and celebrating God's calling for your team.

| LECTIO DIVINA |

Adele Calhoun defines Lectio Divina as a way of reading the Bible for the "sake of a transforming encounter with God."[2] In short, this is a devotional reading of Scripture which aims at slowing us down to hear the word read aloud, to allow the Holy Spirit to draw our attention to some particular aspect in order to hear the ancient Word speaking to us today. Calhoun marks out five movements that we go through while practicing Lectio Divina. They are:

1. Silencio—quiet preparation of the heart. Come into God's presence, slow down, relax, and intentionally release the chaos and noise in your mind to him.
2. Lectio—read the word. Read a Scripture passage slowly and out loud, lingering over the words so that they resonate in your heart. When a word or phrase catches your attention, don't keep reading. Stop and attend to what God is saying to you. Be open

---

2. Adele Calhoun Spiritual Disciplines Handbook, 290.

to the word. Don't analyze it or judge it. Listen and wait (as you do this in a group, read the whole passage and then proceed to the next step).

3. Meditatio—meditate. Read the Scripture a second time out loud. Savor the words. Listen for any invitation that God is extending to you in this word. Reflect on the importance of the words that light up to you ... gently explore the ramifications of God's invitation.

4. Oratio—respond, pray. Read the Scripture a third time. Now is the moment to enter into a personal dialogue with God. There is no right or wrong way to do this. The important thing is to respond truthfully and authentically. What feelings has the text aroused in you? Name where you are resistant or want to push back. Become aware of where you feel invited into a deeper way of being with God. Talk to God about these feelings.

5. Contemplatio—contemplate, rest and wait in the presence of God. Allow some time for the word to sink deeply into your soul. Yield and surrender yourself to God. Before you leave, you might consider a reminder that can help you dwell on or incarnate this word throughout the day.[3]

---

3. Ibid., 168-169.

HEALTHY TEAMS TRUST

| **REFLECTION** | In *Becoming a Healthy Team*, Macchia takes the time to discuss the nature of cooperation and competition.[4] Often, teams are spoken of using military, athletic, or even advertising language. While these things include teams, they are teams which exist in contexts that are very different from our own calling as ministry teams. Sports, business, and military teams exist for their own good whether it is to win battles, games, or market share. What is unique about ministry teams is that our calling is to exist for the good of others. When we are serving our communities well, you might even say that we exist to lose, for in the eyes of the world, we give, sacrifice, and surrender with no thought of the bottom line of our own status or reward. It has been said that "comparison is the thief of joy." It is no less true to say that "competition is the thief of love" for it is almost impossible to truly desire someone's best for them when we are in competition with them. Reflect on the existence of cooperation or competition within your team. How can cooperation be fostered while competition is done away with?

| **BIBLE STUDY** | Read I Samuel 18:7-9. What might have become of Saul had he not allowed jealousy of David to steer the remainder of the course of his life. He used his army more for tracking down David, than for making Israel a safe place to live for his people. How might a partnership between David and Saul have changed the course of history? Read about Saul's son, Jonathan in I Samuel 18:1-4, 19:1-6, 20:1-17, 23:15-18. Why was Jonathan willing to give up his own claim to the throne for David? Have you been a Saul on your team? What would it look like if your team was composed of Jonathan's instead of Saul's?

| **CONFESSION** | Commit right now to confessing any competitive spirit that you have allowed to separate you from a team member. If it has affected the team, confess it to the entire team. If it has only affected that other member, confess it to that member. Often we think of competition as not affecting the work and lives of others, but as an internal reality in our hearts. But the truth is that in competing with a team member we have been unable to fully serve, compliment, assist, and cheer on that person.

---

4.   Macchia, 21-23.

BUILD TRUST THROUGH COMMUNITY

| **BIBLE STUDY** | Read Acts 2:42-47, focusing in primarily on what the early church was doing together. Why are those things significant? Why do you think the early church selected those activities as crucial to their community? Do you think that God intended that one of the outcomes of those activities to be the drawing together of his people? Are these practices present in your team life? What might change if they became more integral to your existence as a team? Finally, what is the source for this exemplary community? How did the work of God at Pentecost make this extraordinary community possible?

| **SHARE** | Reflect upon a past team or community of which you have been a part. Picture the team that you most think about when you think of true community. What made this a blessed community? What activities did the group participate in together? What was the common bond that brought you together?

| **REFLECTION** | Most Christians when reflecting on the above questions recall a small, intimate group which came together in order to pursue Christ. They regularly participated in Bible study, prayer for one another and the world, and accountability. They also spent time just enjoying one another's presence. Some even celebrated the Lord's Supper together. This should not surprise us when we look at Acts 2. It was these activities around which the early Church revolved. Rarely do Christians report their deepest community experiences as coming from a group with little spiritual interest. A social club can be fun, but it seldom results in close community. As you reflect upon Acts 2:42-47 and your own experiences in Christian community, how do you find this to be true?

BUILD TRUST THROUGH CELEBRATION

| **BIBLE STUDY** | Read Acts 2:46-47 and notice the attitudes and dispositions of the community described there. From the surrounding context, discuss why it was that this community spent so much time in celebration and praise together. What do you think it would have been like to be a part of this community? What was it about Pentecost that caused a celebratory people to emerge?

| **REFLECTION** | One of the most time consuming requirements in the Old Testament placed by God upon the people of Israel was the requirement to celebrate. Mere weeks separated festival after festival requiring the people to stop working and start rejoicing, worshipping, remembering, and fellowshipping. The word "feast" appears just under 150 times in the English Bible. It has been said that God commanded the people to party, but they refused.

| ACTIVATE | You must choose to celebrate as a community weekly, monthly, quarterly, or a combination of these. It is your job to discover events or accomplishment worthy of celebration. Perhaps you could compile a list of team birthdays and be intentional about planning lavish celebrations of the life of each team member. You could revisit the Church calendar and celebrate various feast days together. If you are a team leader, few things should be as important to you as noticing great performances by your team and leading in celebration. Make noticing, recording, and acting on these performance recognition events a part of your regular to-do list. Revisit pages 62-63 of Becoming a Healthy Team for ideas of how to pull off an appreciation banquet.

BUILD TRUST THROUGH COMMUNICATION

| FUN | It's time for everyone to present their most embarrassing moment. The challenge here is to share your story as if you were a master storyteller ... embellish your story in such a way as to help your teammates enter into your embarrassment. If your moment occurred in high school, in front of a large group of peers, with the boy/girl that you had a crush on standing nearby, make sure to communicate that. Let them know why you were mortified and help them to share that sense of hilarious dread with you.

| SHARE | Life maps are one of the best ways of getting to know someone else. They can be done is many different ways. Often, you may draw out a timeline of your life and share it that way. You could draw a series of pictures that communicates key points in your life. Sharing your life's story can be daunting, but a good place to start is by identifying 2-3 of the most positive moments of your life and 2-3 of the hardest moments of your life and presenting them in some visual format and then explaining them to your team. Allow each member to share as deeply as they are able. Set aside significant time for this sharing to take place, perhaps as much as an hour per person.

| REFLECTION | This reflection exercise is going to be a little different than others. Instead of reflecting on a quote from someone else, allow each team member to reflect on the life story of the member who is sharing. After a time of reflection, pray for God to enable you to identify with the team member who has just shared. Then allow each team member to ask questions regarding the life map which was shared. Finally, each team member should speak works of identification back to the member who has shared. This is not a time for advice, correction, or interpretation. It is simply a time to say, "I rejoice with you in that wonderful experience that you shared about" or "I'm so sorry that you had to experience that event in your life. I really grieve with you over that."

BUILD TRUST THROUGH CONFLICT

| **SHARE** | In *Becoming a Healthy Team*, Macchia writes, "Families of origin are the dominant teacher in how conflicts get resolved. The role models of parents and extended family members are the first influences we have in shaping our understanding of how to handle conflict."[5] Allow each team member a moment to reflect on how conflict was handled in their families while growing up. Perhaps some in your group are from families that are conflict avoiders, choosing the passive aggressive route to sharing one's opinions. Others, no doubt, are from families who should have made litigation the family business because they are so good at and actually love arguing. Have each team member share about their family models. Allow them to comment on the good, bad, and ugly of that particular approach, and whether they have inherited/implemented that approach to conflict for themselves. What have been the consequences of this?

| **REFLECTION** | Read the following chart which outlines the consequences of failure to enter into constructive conflict within your team. Patrick Lencioni lists "Fear of Conflict" as one of the five top dysfunctions of a team. How are you, as an individual, going to overcome your own fears in this area and how is your team going to come together to make sure that you are allowing the team to flourish to its fullest potential?[6]

Teams that fear conflict	Teams that engage in conflict
Have boring meetings	Have lively, interesting meetings
Create environments were back-channel politics and personal attacks thrive	Extract and exploit the ideas of all team members
Ignore controversial topics that are critical to team success	Solve real problems quickly
Fail to tap into all the opinions and perspectives of team members	Minimize politics
Waste time and energy with posturing and interpersonal risk management	Put critical topics on the table for discussion

---

5.   Macchia, 65.
6.   The chart is taken from Patrick Lencioni, The Five Dysfunctions of a Team, (San Francisco: Jossey-Bass, 2002), 204. We recommend giving copies of this book to your entire team because of the time it gives to illustrate and explain the fruitfulness of team conflict. Lencioni also does a great service to his readers as he takes the time to differentiate between what is good conflict and bad conflict.

TEAM NOTES

Ideas for building TRUST on our team.

HEALTHY TEAMS EMPOWER

| **BIBLE STUDY** | Jesus empowered people for ministry. Read Luke 10:1-20. What kind of tasks were the 72 sent out to accomplish? Were they important tasks? Were they tasks that Jesus was unwilling to do himself? Notice Jesus' words in v. 20. What effect would these words have on the disciples? How do you feel when you read them? Why would Jesus say this to those whom he had empowered for service?

| **SHARE** | Share about an experience at a workplace or as a volunteer in which you felt empowered to accomplish your responsibilities. Similarly, share about an experience when you felt hindered and why. What was it about the teams that you worked with that allowed the good or the bad experiences to take place?

| **REFLECTION** | Pages 80-81 of *Becoming a Healthy Team* explain the acrostic DESIGN which is a tool for helping individual team members understand their gifts, passions, and themselves. As you look over these areas of your life, what DESIGN begins to come to foreground? The following is a short reproduction of DESIGN:

D is for desire. What is your passion? If ... you could do anything in the world for the Lord, what job would you choose to do?

E is for experience. What tasks or projects have influenced you in the past? What have you learned from the times when you have been hurt? How have they made you more compassionate toward others in similar situations?

S is for spiritual gift. God sent his Spirit, who distributed gifts to the church through which we would carry on his work. What are your spiritual gifts?

I is for individual style. Each of us has a unique temperament (extrovert/introvert) ... that will not change your calling as a Christian, but it will tell you how to carry out your calling.

G is for growth phase. Are you an infant, toddler, adolescent, young adult, or a mature adult in your relationship with Christ?

N is for natural abilities. What do you enjoy doing? When we minister within our design, life gets exciting and fun.

EMPOWER THROUGH GIFTS AND PASSIONS

| FUN | Each person in the group should answer aloud the following questions. Perhaps allowing each person to answer the first question and then proceeding to the next one and so forth: What was your childhood dream career? If you could go anywhere for vacation, where would it be and why? What would you say is your wildest dream? If you were to retire early but still desired to work, what two career paths might you choose? If you could choose to have the skill to make or fix anything, what would it be? Finally, you need a new name, make up one of the most outlandish names for yourself. Create nametags using these names and call one another by these names for the rest of your time together.

| ACTIVATE | As a team, take at least one spiritual gifts or personality inventory. If you can do one of each, it would be most beneficial as spiritual gifts are exercised differently depending on one's temperament.

One assessment that has been used successfully among teams can be found at www.leadingfromyourstrengths.com. It is a quick assessment and provides 28 pages of easy to understand analysis. For help walking through the assessments as a team, you might want to purchase a copy of Leading from Your Strengths by Rodney Cox and Eric Tooker. Another assessment used frequently in spiritual formation work is the Enneagram which delves deeply into 9 profiles, indentifying one's primary personality style with its particular challenges to Christian maturity. It clarifies the primary way one engages relationships and offers ways one can cultivate healthy relational interaction with God and others. Call us at (877) TEAM-LTI for more on the Enneagram.

| RETREAT | Plan a weekend retreat in which you will walk through each team members' assessment one by one. Use the information provided by the assessment to plot charts of team members' gifts and personalities. Talk through what is revealed by these charts. Are team giftings diverse or not? What are the strengths and weaknesses of where personalities were plotted? How might this strengthen or hinder the team? How can you capitalize on all of the gifts and personalities of the team? Afterward, choose one project that the team is working on or has coming up in the near future, and with all that you've learned about one another in mind, put those strengths to work for God. Keep these principles in mind from Cox and Tooker:

1. Understand your own God-given strengths. "This is a key to ... finding your place on the team where God has placed you."
2. Recognize and respect the God-given strengths of those you work with. "This is a key to the commitment of each team member to each other."

3. Blend those differences to accomplish your task. "This results in greater effectiveness and productivity for your team."[7]

EMPOWER THROUGH DEFINED RESPONSIBILITIES

| **SHARE** | On a 3x5 note card write out the name of each team member including yourself. Beside their name, write out what you understand the responsibilities of that team member to be. Shuffle the cards and have the leader read the cards out loud. Ask each team member to respond to the descriptions about themselves. Were there individuals whose job descriptions seemed to be hard to identify? Were some individuals' descriptions extremely narrow or wide when compared with reality? What other interesting things came out of these descriptions?

| **CONFESSION** | It is easy to understand that the "worst thing to do to another team member is to give him or her a job without the accompanying authority to perform it."[8] Indeed, responsibility without authority breeds frustration. Reflect on the areas of team life and ministry for which you feel responsible but for which you unable to do anything about for lack of authority. After a time of prayer asking for understanding and love, openly share these with the team. As each member shares, focus not on who might be causing the frustration but on each member's desire to serve well in areas for which they feel responsible. Allow this to lead into a time of determining if the areas for which members feel responsible are actually their responsibility. If members know that they are not responsible for a particular task yet carry a burden of responsibility in that area, try to understand why they feel that way. Is it because their passions and gifts really fit that area better than the one in which they serve? Is it because they care about the person responsible for that area and are concerned that they are able to succeed?

| **DISCIPLINE** | As a team, memorize each other's list of responsibilities. This may not include the minuscule details of a person's daily schedule, but you should be able to agree on and clearly communicate what it is that makes each team member vital to the task to which you are called. These descriptions might also contain non-professional responsibilities such as "Jeff is responsible to make us laugh daily." Take time to define the unique role which is assumed by each equally unique person and commit together to know them.

---

7. Rodney Cox and Eric Tooker, Leading from Your Strengths: Building Close-Knit Ministry Teams, (Nashville: Broadman and Holman Nashville, 2004), 7.
8. Macchia, 70.

EMPOWER THROUGH TEACHABILITY AND RESOURCING

| BIBLE STUDY | The Proverbs are full of exhortations that God's people be teachable. That means receiving correction and rebuke well. It also means surrounding ourselves with Godly counselors. Read the following Proverbs: 1:5, 1:7, 4:5, 11:2, 11:14, 12:15, 13:10, 15:22, 16:16, 17:10, 19:20, 24:6, 27:9, 28:23. What is the result of the lack of counselors? What is the result of not accepting Godly correction? Why do you think it is so difficult to accept rebuke or advice? Who are the people in your life serving as counselors for you? Are they worthy people? Read I Kings 12:1-17. What was Rehoboam's downfall? Why did he listen to his young advisors instead of the advisors of his father? How might the history of Israel been different if he had accepted the advice of the elders? What might we be saying about Rehoboam today if he had answered the people wisely instead of rashly?

| SHARE | After a few moments of reflection, each member should identify one area of their ministry in which they would like to develop, whether it is administrative, people, or ministry skills. No area is off the table as we look to serve the Lord to the best of our ability. Share why you feel the need to gain further training, education, and/or skills in that area.

| ACTIVATE | It is time to gather options for growth in the areas identified above. There has been much written regarding the need to be a life long learner and even a learning organization.[9] Scour the internet and other resources for information on courses, workshops, conferences, books, and other opportunities for training and education in those areas. As a team, talk through ways that the team or organization could aid each member in acquiring the training and education that they need, whether they just need paid days off to go to a conference or they need help with tuition for a class. Sometimes investing in its people is the wisest use of money for any organization.

EMPOWER THROUGH DELEGATION AND ACCOUNTABILITY

| FUN | For this exercise you will need a blindfold for each member of the team and a long rope or string tied into a circle. While blindfolded, the team must take the rope and attempt to form a trapezoid with it. Once the team thinks that they have accomplished their goal, take off the blind folds and observe how well you did.

| SHARE | While still gathered around the trapezoid, begin to reflect on the role that each member assumed during the activity. Who became the leader? Who zoned out? Who just wanted to take directions and help? Were you the trapezoid expert who had to

---

9.   Steve Moore in his book The Dream Cycle, helps Christians to identify areas for growth and then to plan in order to accomplish that growth. The Fifth Discipline by Peter Senge discusses the need for organizations as a whole to be learning organizations.

explain exactly what kind of a shape it was? How were these roles delegated? How did being blindfolded affect the way that you communicated? Notice how you felt not being able to see what each other was doing. Did you find yourself using hand motions and pointing in directions and then realizing that no one could see you? Now share about an instance on your ministry team in which you felt blindfolded. What was the cause of that feeling? Was it a communication issue? What is a lack of clear delegation? Discuss how delegation takes place in your ministry team. Is the team leader just passing on jobs that he or she disdains? Are team members' gifts and passions the driving force behind their assigned responsibilities?

| REFLECTION | Accountability can be a hard pill to swallow; however, as a ministry team, you have collective goals to accomplish, and one member can cause the entire team to fail to meet those goals. Jesus expected accountability. We read in Matthew 18:15-18 that Jesus instructs the disciples in accountability. They (and we) were commanded to hold each other to God's standard. A team member's failure may not be sin or even as a result of poor work, but sometimes that failure is due to issues that could have been controlled. It is important to talk about every missed goal to determine the cause, be it irresponsibility, miscommunication, or lack of delegation. Rick Love argues that there are 3 primary reasons for Church discipline: For the glory of God, for the purity of the Church, and for the restoration of the sinner.[10] Similarly, accountability on a team has three goals: For the glory of God, for the sake of the team's purpose, and for the unity of the team. By entering into discussions of accountability, and perhaps confession, we will be forced to remember Who we are serving as a team, what we as a team exist to do, and which relationships within the team have been strained through this incident. How are you as a team going to put in place structures that will allow you to hold each other accountable for the glory of God and the good of the team?

---

10. Rick Love, Peacemaking, (Pasadena, William Carey Publishers, 2003).

TEAM NOTES

Ideas for increasing EMPOWERMENT on our team.

HEALTHY TEAMS ASSIMILATE

| **LECTIO DIVINA** | Read, again, the sign-post description of the discipline of Lectio Divina. Work through these steps by reading I Corinthians 12 as rendered in *Becoming a Healthy Team*:

The team is a unit, though it is made up of many parts; and though all its parts are many, they form one team. So it is with Christ. For we were all baptized by one Spirit into one team—whether Jews or Greeks, slave or free—and we were all given the one Spirit to drink. Now the team is not made up on one part but of many. If the foot should say, "Because I am not a hand, I do not belong to the team," it would not for that reason cease to be part of the team. And if the ear should say, "Because I am not an eye, I do not belong to the team," it would not for that reason cease to be part of the team. If the whole team were an eye, where would the sense of hearing be? If the whole team were an ear, where would the sense of smell be? But in fact God has arranged the parts of the team, every one of them, just as he wanted them to be. If they were all one part, where would the team be? As it is, there are many parts, but one team. The eye cannot say to the hand, "I don't need you!" And the head cannot say to the feet, "I don't need you!" On the contrary, those parts of the team that seem to be weaker are indispensable, and the parts that we think are less honorable we treat with special honor. And the parts that are unpresentable are treated with special modesty, while our presentable parts need not special treatment. But God has combined the members of the team and has given greater honor to the parts that lacked it, so that there should be no division in the team, but that its parts should have equal concern for each other. If one part suffers, every part suffers with it; if one part is honored, every part rejoices with it. Now you are the team of Christ, and each one of you is a part of it. And in the church God has appointed first of all apostles, second prophets, third teachers, then workers of miracles, also those having gifts of healing, those able to help others, those with gifts of administration, and those speaking in different kinds of tongues. Are all apostles? Are all prophets? Are all teachers? Do all work miracles? Do all have gifts of healing? Do all speak in tongues? Do all interpret? But eagerly desire the greater gifts. And now I will show you the most excellent way ... [11]

---

11. Macchia, Becoming a Healthy Team, 31-33.

ASSIMILATE THROUGH CROSS-POLLINATION

| **REFLECTION** | In his bestselling book *The Five Dysfunctions of a Team*, Patrick Lencioni lists "fear of conflict" as one of the dysfunctions that will derail any team. The reason that this dysfunction is so crucial is that the unique giftings on the team are unharnessed unless there is the opportunity for true collaboration. And true collaboration of variously gifted and impassioned people will not always be smooth sailing. Macchia writes that it is in "the intersection of ideas, lives, and ministry responsibilities, the team creates their 'music.' There is a bit of a push-pull going on to produce the new sound, but after much practice, the tempo and lyrics are brought beautifully together."[12] How is your team doing at cross-pollination? Does each member know not only their responsibilities, but the responsibilities of their team members? Does each member have input into the areas that are under the leadership of another team member? Do you invite a wide array of individuals to speak into your work from their unique and informed point of view?

| **SHARE** | Each member of the team should share about a project that they are currently working on. Be sure to explain what problem is being solved or goal being met by the accomplishment of this project. You might even find, after reflection together, that a particular project does nothing to accomplish a goal or solve a problem, but that it has become busy work or an attempt to use resources just because they exist. After each member shares, allow the rest of the team to ask questions about the project, goal, problem, etc. Ask each member to share how that project might intersect or affect the areas of ministry which they oversee. Then invite each member to look at the project critically coming up with at least one constructive and loving criticism of the project as it currently stands and one positive comment regarding the same project. Then discern as a team how the collective energies in the room might bring greater momentum to the project.

| **ACTIVATE** | This activity might be difficult for the team leader, but can provide unique insights into their leadership and the team make-up. Allow each team member to direct a weekly team meeting. As the team leader, you should be taking notes on how the meeting is different under each team member than under yourself. Notice how certain issues are raised up as important and others lowered in importance depending on who is leading. Notice how each member invites or blocks feedback. Notice what icebreakers or conversation starters are employed. Notice the atmosphere of the team as they go through a meeting under new facilitators. Does the rest of the team seem more relaxed than usual? Are some team members participating more or less than usual? Are all of the topics that you find important getting raised? If not, ask yourself why particular team members felt no need to address those issues?

---

12. Macchia, 93.

ASSIMILATE THROUGH OTHERS-ORIENTATION

| **REFLECTION** | Philippians 2:1-11 has been held up regularly at the foremost passage concerning the need for others-orientation. We are told to follow the example of Christ in placing the will of the Father and the needs of the world above his own wants. If ever a passage was meant to be embodied by believers, it is this passage. Walk through the steps of the discipline of Lectio Divina together and share with one another regarding the areas of the passage that are finding resonance with you.

| **LECTIO DIVINA** | From the above Philippians passage, we know that Christ was God, but that he emptied himself of his own divine right in order to be a servant to all. To sum up, Jesus was God, but behaved as a man in perfect submission to the rule of the Father. Throughout the Old Testament, we see the exact opposite in the actions of men and women. All one need do is read Daniel 4:4-37, Ezekiel 28:1-10, and Genesis 3:1-19 among other passages to see this play out. Nebuchadnezzar, the king of Tyre, and Adam and Eve, all of whom were human, attempted to raise themselves up to the realm of deity. Nebuchadnezzar said that it is he who built Babylon by the might of his own power and glory. The king of Tyre boldly claimed that he was a god, and of course, Adam and Eve ate of the fruit believing that when they did, they would become like God. While the divine Christ submitted to the Father, created mankind has continued to try and dethrone God in a feeble attempt at spiritual coup d'*état*. That is the beauty of Jesus. He accomplishes for the Father and for sinful man, what mankind has ever been unable to do. Take some time to enter into prayerful worship of Jesus, the perfectly divine God and the perfectly humble man. Finish your time of worship asking the Father to reveal to you areas in team life where you need to assume a posture of greater servanthood towards your teammates as you pursue greater submission to God.

ASSIMILATE THROUGH SYSTEMIC DIRECTION

| **REFLECTION** | To think systemically, one must begin by remembering that it is not just individuals that affect our society, but the systems that are put in place. The easiest place to look to understand this is the government. Anytime lobbyist groups are able to push congress to pass bills to their advantage, competing lobbyists are disadvantaged. From this point onward, it is not an individual that disadvantages them, but the system. It is now a law, meaning that the system itself has stacked the cards in favor of one group and against another. Now reflect on your own organization and team. What fail-safe, value, or procedure is in place to allow certain things to happen at the expense of something else? This is not always a bad thing, but we want to be aware of how our bureaucracy and red tape affects each area of team and organizational life. Can you think of any

established norms that need to be revisited together which might nurture team life or greater efficiency? Take some time to share these thoughts as a team and collectively assess the need for change.

| **RETREAT** | The most important systemic direction which you will receive as a team are housed in the team vision, mission, and value statements. If you are currently developing these statements which represent the soul of the organization or team, or if you have inherited these from your superiors, one of the best things you can do as a team is to retreat together. If you are unclear about or uncommitted to your mission, vision, and values, then you will never be able to accomplish God's will for your team. At the very least, during the retreat, your team will want to begin to establish its vision, mission, and goals. To lack any of the three is sure to derail your team.[13]

- **Vision** describes your overall purpose for existence.
- **Mission** is a focused guidance that helps you determine the unique way in which you have been called to fulfill the vision.
- **Values** are the principles and standards that define what is right, desirable, and worthwhile.

After discovering the above, you must apply them to your ministry …

> … by converting the concept of a preferable reality into a series of specific goals (measurable outcomes that relate to the mission, vision, and values), strategies (general approaches designed to facilitate the accomplishment of the specified goals), and tactics (specific actions that relate to the strategies undertaken to achieve specific goals).

Many of the activities found in the "Healthy Teams Manage" section of this workbook will benefit your retreat time. Be sure to explore any information that will benefit you during that time.

ASSIMILATE THROUGH MINISTRY MULTIPLICATION

| **REFLECTION** | In John 17:4 Jesus prays, "I glorified You on the earth, having accomplished the work which You have given Me to do." What is interesting about this statement is when it was prayed. Jesus is in the Garden of Gethsemane. He has yet to go to the cross, rise from the dead, or ascend into heaven. Nevertheless, Jesus asserts that he has "accomplished" (notice the past tense) the work which the Father had given him. What

---

13. The following is a distillation and modification of information from George Barna's The Power of Team Leadership, 37-62. I recommend your entire team read through Barna's full chapter on vision as preparation for the retreat. You will notice that what we call "Vision," Barna calls "Mission" and vice versa.

work might Jesus be referring to? The context of this is the "High Priestly" prayer in which Jesus goes on to spend the remainder of the conversation talking about the disciples and those that would believe through them, so it is no stretch to assume that Jesus is talking about the work of multiplying himself in the lives of these disciples. Allow that to sink in. The Father was greatly glorified by Jesus' work of multiplication. The disciples are the result of the work assigned to Jesus by the Father, but not only the disciples, but also those who would believe through their word (John 17:20). That includes us. Are you also passing on the word? Who is it that you are specifically helping to raise up to full maturity in Christ and ministry?

| **SHARE** | Share why you are here … why you are a part of this ministry team. More than that, why are you in ministry at all? Who was it that first inspired or challenged you to consider allowing God to use you in ministry? Where were you? What were the steps between that first sense of calling and your current ministry?

| **DISCIPLINE** | As a team, memorize 2 Timothy 2:2 which reads, "The things which you have heard from me in the presence of many witnesses, entrust these to faithful men who will be able to teach others also." Notice the number of generations which are mentioned by Paul. Jesus and Paul both felt the pressing need to multiply themselves. You might even consider adding ministry multiplication to your personal and team values.

TEAM NOTES

Ideas for greater ASSIMILATION across our team.

_____
_____
_____
_____
_____
_____
_____
_____
_____
_____
_____
_____
_____
_____
_____
_____
_____
_____
_____
_____
_____
_____
_____
_____
_____
_____
_____
_____
_____
_____
_____

HEALTHY TEAMS MANAGE

| **SHARE** | Have each member of the team share about one team, group, etc that they have loved to manage. To help them begin thinking, here are examples of "teams" that they may have managed before: Little League Baseball/Softball, Boy/Girl Scouts, Book Club, Fantasy Football Team, Church Committee, Knitting Club, a weekly get-together such as a Dinner Club or a group that meets to watch the local sports team together, etc. What did they enjoy about managing these groups? What did they not enjoy?

| **REFLECTION** | "We manage things, but we lead people."[14] I found this out the hard way while leading my first team. One of my assignments as team leader was to choose a book that we would read together as a team and talk about during our weekly meeting. My creative juices got the best of me as I decided to assign a different book to each team member. I thought to myself, "These are unique individuals and so we need to each read a unique book for maximum growth." And who, besides myself, was qualified to tell each member what book they should read? I diagnosed each member's "issues" and assigned a book to "treat" them. In doing this, not only did I treat them like patients in a hospital instead of fully qualified members of a ministry, but I also failed to see how important it was for the team to read and converse about the same material together. It was the one time each week where we got to unite around some topic, and I took that opportunity away. Instead of team unity, my actions as team leader resulted in further distance between team members. Are there times when you have been a part of a poorly managed team? Perhaps you were the manager. What lessons are crucial to learn from those experiences?

| **ACTIVATE** | "Actually, the goal of management is to help others self-manage, teaching them the principles and practices that will make this possible, including time management, setting priorities, stewardship of resources, and seeing tasks through to completion."[15]Remembering that we lead people and manage things, who are you responsible for preparing to manage the things that God has given them? How have you done at preparing them to do their job well? Remember that their performance reflects upon the one by whom they were trained. Place yourself in their position, and score yourself 1-5 on the

---

14. Macchia, 102.
15. Ibid.

following questions:

1. Did I allow them to ask all of their questions? Did I give them enough of my time?
2. Did I address each of their responsibilities, showing how something can be done, but allowing freedom in their personal approach? Do I micromanage their efforts?
3. Would I trust them to accomplish the most important of assignments?

How did you score? What do you need to do now?

MANAGE THROUGH STRATEGIC PLANS

| **ACTIVATE** | Henry and Richard Blackaby write concerning spiritual leaders:

Being proactive by nature, leaders want to rush into action. As a result, they don't spend enough time seeking to hear clearly from God. Instead, they simply have a cursory moment of prayer and then begin making their plans. They seek out a few relevant Scriptures and hurry into the goal-setting phase, falsely confident that because they incorporated prayer and Scripture into their goal-setting process, their plans are 'of God.' [16]

They argue that Christian leaders make their plans the same way that secular leaders do, namely, through a list of pros and cons and the selection of the most logical answer, [17]instead of seeking the face of God and listening for his voice to reveal his plans. They are quick to distinguish between what they call "vision" and "revelation." Vision is a plan created by man, but God's plan must be revealed.[18] Steve Macchia, similarly, says that "Listening to the Master's voice together is the work of spiritual discernment … In all effective ministry planning, leaders must discern God's voice."[19] Following is a process for spiritual discernment developed by Ignatius.[20] Each step should be done slowly, in a genuine spirit of waiting on and receiving from God. Linger in prayer together, praying over what has arisen throughout each step and asking for God's wisdom. Prioritization is done throughout to keep the first things first.

1. Assemble the facts. Prioritize them.
    a. PRAY

2. Critique and review options that emerge from facts. Prioritize them.
    a. PRAY

---

16. Henry and Richard Blackaby, Spiritual Leadership, (Nashville: Broadman and Holman, 2001), 70.
17. Ibid, 179.
18. Ibid, 69.
19. Macchia, Becoming a Healthy Team, 108.
20. This material has been modified by Steve Macchia.

3. State reasons why not to consider each option. Prioritize them.
   a. PRAY

4. State reasons why to say yes to each option. Prioritize them.
   a. PRAY

5. Deliberate openly, honestly, and without judgment of one another or drawing a conclusion one way or the other.
   a. PRAY

6. Decide and proceed with next steps.
   a. PRAY

Then,

1. Conduct ongoing evaluations and reviews.
2. Commence process all over again if needed.

MANAGE THROUGH SMART GOALS

| REFLECTION | Paul was a strategic planner. His letters are full of statements regarding his reason for existence (Vision) and his strategic plans (Goals). He constantly reminds his readers that his calling is that of the apostle to the Gentiles, and so calling Gentiles to Christ is the "Vision" for his life. In Romans, we see hints of his goals in statements like 15:19-23, 28. Paul's vision of reaching the Gentiles for Christ was played out through the planting of one or two churches in major cities in every Roman province. He did not intend on sharing the Gospel with every single Gentile, but that the churches which were planted would be the Gospel bearers in each province. He was so sure of his vision and so strategic in his planning that he could say that from Jerusalem to Illyricum, the Gospel had been fully preached! Oh, that the Church today would be so strategic!

| SHARE | Having vision, mission, and value statements without SMART goals is like a sports team with a sign reading "Win the Championship this Year" but never developing a game plan. When they take the field, they have no idea what they are doing, except trying to win a championship. In ministry, this is like having the goal "Advance the Kingdom of God." This is an awesome vision, but where does one begin? Great vision without application results in futility. In Becoming a Healthy Team, SMART goals are defined as "the qualitative and quantitative objectives that you believe God wants you to accomplish together. They are the concrete ways you will measure ministry effectiveness and monitor your planning process in fulfillment of your overall ministry strategy."[21] If vision is the

---

21. Macchia, 113.

engine of your ministry car, then SMART goals are the map detailing exactly how you are going to get to your destination. Remember that SMART stands for:

- Specific
- Measurable
- Achievable
- Results-Oriented
- Time-Dated

It is time to have a discussion about your goals. If you have not already established your ministry vision, mission, and values, then you will need to work through the Assimilate through Systemic Direction activity. After establishing your Vision, Mission, and Values, the logical and necessary next step is to establish SMART goals. Go through your Vision and Mission statement carefully together, one phrase at a time. As you do so, answer the question, "What steps are we taking to achieve this?" You will likely find that some of the things you are already doing meet the criteria of SMART goals, while others do not. Remember that you are called to fulfill God's desires, not to think up something to keep you busy; therefore, you will want to work through the discernment exercise under Manage through Strategic Plans with each phrase of your key statements. As you begin to sense God's direction, ask yourself how the plans that are coming together meet the 5 criteria of SMART goals.

MANAGE THROUGH SYSTEMATIC ADMINISTRATION

| FUN | Find a picture or painting that is hanging in a place where each team member has most likely seen it hundreds of times. Sometimes this is in the lobby area of an office or above the copier or water fountain. For some teams that are spread abroad geography, think of an image that the team should be very familiar with. It might be the front of the building out of which the organization is headquartered. Once you have your image in mind, supply paper and pens to your team, and ask them to recreate the picture or image that you have selected. For instance: "From memory, on this piece of paper, in as much detail as you can, draw the front entrance of our organizational headquarters (or the fake Monet in the hallway)." Afterwards, take the team to stand in front of the picture or entrance and ask them how they did in including details in their sketch. If your organization was run with the same eye for detail as they included in their sketch, how effective would the organization be? Very effective or disastrous?

| **BIBLE STUDY** | How important are details for an organization or the Church? The early church had its own administrative problems. Read Acts 6:1-7. Identify the overlooked detail and the process undertaken by the leadership of the Jerusalem church to deal with that issue? What responsibility was given to those chosen to administrate the food distribution? Do you think they felt empowered to do what they were assigned? At first glance, verse 7 seems to introduce a new idea, but imagine what the possible effects on the ministry would have been if they had not dealt with this issue of food distribution. Can one overlooked area affect an entire movement?

| **ACTIVATE** | Often organizations or teams have one or two individuals that carry the administrative load for everyone so that others on the team might focus their time elsewhere. This can be a great picture of the body working in its strengths; however, those who are continually in administration can feel disconnected from the rest of the ministry because other members do not necessarily make it a point to share successes, failures, joys, and losses with them. They are working harder than anyone else to keep the team or organization running smoothly, but last to hear the news of a goal achieved or a mission accomplished. Each team member should figure out a way to bless those in administration through reporting to them what God is doing in their areas of responsibility on the team (which is made possible by their great administrative care). Those in administration should be encouraged to share what their day to day looks like so that the rest of the team can appreciate the work that they do. Finally, as a team, continue to come up with creative ways to bless and encourage those working on the details. This can be done through notes, cards, lunch parties, and heaps of praise during staff meetings. Their success, like the deacons of Jerusalem, is what will enable the team vision to continue to move forward.

MANAGE THROUGH RESULTS EVALUATION

| **FUN** | This may seem a little hokey, but it is just a little activity to get you eased into the topic of evaluation. First, take your team to a local museum. You are going to choose 10 pieces of art which you will each evaluate. Give each member a note pad on which to "score" the agreed upon pieces of art. At each piece of art, allow one of the team members, who will pretend to be the artist, to share their "vision" for the painting and what they were trying to communicate. Next, allow the rest of the team (i.e. the art experts) to critique each piece of art. Each person should record scores of 1-10 in the areas of Creativity, Execution, and Wow Factor. Tally up the scores and crown a champion. For the extra silly team, perhaps you could even present your findings to some of the museum staff. Afterwards, have team members answer the following questions.

1. How did you feel as you evaluated the artwork?
2. What is usually more difficult for you, to evaluate someone's work or to have your own work evaluated? Why?
3. What do you feel are crucial aspects of giving constructive criticism?

| LECTIO DIVINA | Perform the steps described in the Team Activities & Exercises section for the discipline of Lectio Divina using the Parable of the Talents from Matthew 25:14-30 as your passage.

| REFLECTION | In *Becoming a Healthy Team*, Macchia writes:

Creating simple evaluation tools that assess the vitality of your team or your ministry will help you see where you are strong and where you need to improve … A leader and team that are open to evaluation make a strong statement to those they serve. They are expressing an openness to learn, grow, change, and monitor progress and are showing others that no team or ministry is ever "complete" in its intention or execution. When teams do self-evaluations, they embody the transformational process of growth and maturity. In essence they are modeling what it means to be a teachable disciple of Jesus Christ, as well as a discerning team that desires more than anything else to be in the exact epicenter of God's will.[22]

Is this a current reality in your team? Are there evaluation tools in place designed to help your team perform at its best? Is there anything standing in the way of this happening? Is the trust level of the team high enough for peer evaluation to occur? If not, what are you going to do about it to build deeper trust?

---

22. Macchia, 115.

TEAM NOTES

Ideas for better MANAGEMENT within our team processes.

HEALTHY TEAMS SERVE

| **LECTIO DIVINA** | Practice the discipline of Lectio Divina together on the following passage, taken from John 13:4-17 in The Message:

Jesus knew that the Father had put him in complete charge of everything, that he came from God and was on his way back to God. So he got up from the supper table, set aside his robe, and put on an apron. Then he poured water into a basin and began to wash the feet of the disciples, drying them with his apron. When he got to Simon Peter, Peter said, "Master, you wash my feet?"

Jesus answered, "You don't understand now what I'm doing, but it will be clear enough to you later."

Peter persisted, "You're not going to wash my feet—ever!"

Jesus said, "If I don't wash you, you can't be part of what I'm doing."

"Master!" said Peter. "Not only my feet, then. Wash my hands! Wash my head!"

Jesus said, "If you've had a bath in the morning, you only need your feet washed now and you're clean from head to toe. My concern, you understand, is holiness, not hygiene. So now you're clean. But not every one of you." (He knew who was betraying him. That's why he said, "Not every one of you.")

After he had finished washing their feet, he took his robe, put it back on, and went back to his place at the table. Then he said, "Do you understand what I have done to you? You address me as 'Teacher' and 'Master,' and rightly so. That is what I am. So if I, the Master and Teacher, washed your feet, you must now wash each other's feet. I've laid down a pattern for you. What I've done, you do. I'm only pointing out the obvious. A servant is not ranked above his master; an employee doesn't give orders to the employer. If you understand what I'm telling you, act like it--and live a blessed life.

SERVE THROUGH HEARTFELT PRAYER

| **ACTIVATE** | Following are just a sampling of prayer practices that you might consider:

1. Assign prayer partners on the team who will commit to sharing weekly prayer needs with each other and spending one-on-one time in conversation over lunch once a month. This can be one simple way to stimulate hearts of prayer among your team.

2. Another practice that a team might adopt is intercessory prayer for the world. You may not serve on a team of missionaries, but you do serve a missionary God who is redeeming all nations. Go to www.operationworld.org. Each day, a different country is highlighted. You are provided with ample prayer fodder through demographics, socio-political snapshots, the status of Christianity in that country, and specific prayer requests. When an organization prays, they typically pray for one another and those that they minister to directly. By praying for nations that your organization might never minister in, you are declaring that it is God's agenda that matters most, not our team's or organization's. He has given us a ministry, but we remember that we make up one small part of what God is accomplishing throughout the world.

3. One final practice that you might consider is praying for other ministries that have very similar visions/missions to your own. Again, these organizations are not our competition, but our brothers and sisters. As they serve in similar ways as we do, we might even begin to see them as members of the same body working side by side to accomplish God's goals in your area of ministry.

| **REFLECTION** | In the summer of 2000, I went to China. In my mind, I had four weeks to reach 1 Billion people. Pretty grand expectations, I know. It did not take long for me to become bitter. I was bitter at the missionary hosting me because he wasn't getting me into the thick of things, allowing me to "really minister!" I was bitter with the Chinese people who didn't speak my language. I was bitter with God because if he would have opened the right doors, I could have reached China. I just needed to be able to speak with more people. Two weeks into my time there, God began to silently and softly rebuke me. It was as if he was trying to say, "Justin, do you really think that you can do more for China by talking to the people than by talking to me about the people?" It was as if scales had fallen from my eyes. Hudson Taylor, founder of China Inland Mission, once said that "when man works, man works, but when man prays, God works." If anything of lasting value was going to take place in China because of my time there, it was going to be because I went before my all-powerful, heavenly Father on behalf of its people. Those last two weeks were a mountain top experience. I had no thought of my reaching China, but I had every hope that God would reach China. After two weeks of sweet intercession, I left China knowing that an eternal impact was made, not through work, but through prayer. What about your team? Who are you relying on to accomplish God's goals? Are you relying on yourself? Donors? Good resources and publications?

SERVE THROUGH DISCERNMENT OF NEED

| **REFLECTION** | Reflect on and discuss this extended quote taken from Reuben Job's *A Guide to Spiritual Discernment*. Allow that discussion to lead into a time of prayer ... for one another, for the world, and for God's will to be done in and through the little piece of his will that your team is called to see manifested in the world.

We don't need to look to the other side of the world or country or even the other side of our town to find signs of brokenness. Careful self-examination reveals the fractures deep in our own lives. These wounds, old and new, also cry out for healing.

The cries of the broken world are all around us and within us. How can these cries be heard as the voice of God? How can the world's brokenness be a sign of God's vision for a new heaven and a new earth?

Those who have gone before us along the pathway of discernment, seeking only God's will and way, remind us that dissatisfaction with things as they are is one essential element in discovering God's will ...

... Dissatisfaction with things as they are is one of the ways that we invite the coming of God's reign in our midst.

A second characteristic of those who are able to discern God's will is a passion for God's will. Along with dissatisfaction with things as they are is the yearning for what can be.

Another quality of the person or community that is able to hear God's voice and to see God's vision is the capacity to remain open to God. To read the scriptures, to listen to the cries of the world, including our own hearts, to immerse ourselves in prayer, and to act quickly when we sense God calling us to some simple or profound witness or service ... The One who promised never to leave us also promises to assist us, and therein is our hope.

| **SHARE** | It is easy to get overwhelmed with all of the needs in our church or ministry. Similarly, it is easy to set a program in motion to serve a real need and to never think twice about whether it is indeed meeting that need. As a team, revisit the programs that are currently running in your church or ministry. Ask yourself honest questions regarding the effectiveness of those programs. Is it time to tweak, remove, or add a ministry? Remember that you are called to serve God's agenda, and do not have the luxury of clinging to programs that are not furthering the Kingdom. You may notice how meeting needs requires so many of the other vital traits of leadership like discernment, evaluation, and accountability. Press into the fullness of team vitality as you challenge yourselves to meet real needs.

SERVE THROUGH FULFILLMENT OF CALL

| SHARE | Just today in a conversation, I was reminded about the true nature of calling, namely that we are called to relationship and holiness. Look at passages such as Acts 6:3-8, Titus 1:5-10, I Tim 3:1-13 for the requirement for elders and deacons. People who are chosen or called out of the Church for special service are those who are walking in Godliness, purity, wisdom, and a servant's heart. The spirit is the one who calls them out (Acts 13:1-4). Often, when we talk about calling, we talk about what we are going to do with our lives, but the Bible has a different thing in mind ... not what we do, but who we are. Perhaps we are getting the cart before the horse. We want to find our niche and maybe we'll work on spiritual formation along the way, but for God, spiritual formation is the way to our calling. Take some time for each team member to honestly express where they are at in their spiritual journey. Perhaps they are right on track in ministry and professionally, but things are not going quite as well as they'd like spiritually. After each team member shares, enter into a time where the rest of the team does the following:

1. Speak back to the person who shared what you heard them saying. This is not a time of judgment, advice, or direction. Let us make sure that we heard them correctly by repeating themes, words, or attitudes that we heard or felt from their sharing.
2. Now share how you felt inside as the team member was sharing their situation. Were you burdened, excited, or frustrated? Did what they shared really resonate deeply with you?
3. Then spend some time seeking the Lord for words of encouragement for the team member. Perhaps it's a Scripture or the sense the God is about to do a great work in them. Let us speak life and hope from God to them. Occasionally, a word of correction or exhortation would be appropriate, but we still want to avoid making this into a teaching time.

| REFLECTION | Steve Macchia describes Jesus' ministry through the heart which Christ expressed on earth.[23] Christ expressed a beloved heart. Christ, unlike so many of us, never worried about whether the Father took pleasure in him. He also expressed a broken heart. Christ knew what it was like to hurt and agonize. Jesus found comfort by taking these weaknesses to the Father. The writer of the book of Hebrews says that it was through these sufferings that Jesus was prepared to become our perfect High Priest who could identify with all of our weaknesses. Finally, Jesus expressed a blessed heart. Jesus, beloved and broken, knew what a blessing it was to be the Father's servant. How often he would talk about communion with the Father. It was Jesus source and blessing out of which he

---

23. Macchia, 139-144.

ministered mightily. It is the Father's good pleasure that assures us that we are beloved, speaks tenderly to our brokenness, and bestows his blessings on us. Do you feel beloved, broken, and blessed? If beloved, how has the Father communicated that to you? If broken, how are you allowing the Father to speak into those places? If blessed, in what ways? Take some moments to reflect on these three expressions of the heart of Christ and on how they are manifesting themselves in your own life and ministry. When you reflect on your calling, do these characteristics come to mind?

SERVE THROUGH TRANSFORMATION OF LIFE

| **DISCIPLINE** | Henri Nouwen was asked to speak on Spiritual Leadership in the 21st Century. Upon reflection, he saw that Christians are not called to know the future but to walk with God in the present:

I also came to see that I should not worry about tomorrow, next week, next year or the next century. The more willing I was to look honestly at what I was thinking and saying and doing now, the more easily I would come into touch with the movement of God's Spirit in me, leading me to the future. God is a god of the present and reveals to those who are willing to listen carefully to the moment in which they live the steps they are to take toward the future. 'Do not worry about tomorrow,' Jesus says, 'tomorrow will take care of itself. Each day has enough trouble of its own' (Matt 6:34). [24]

Jesus instead, taught his disciples to follow his lead in doing whatever the Father was doing. What speaker on leadership in the 21st Century could have foreseen the tragic events of 9/11? The world was turned upside down on that day. Wars have ensued. The economy was affected. The people of the world feel less safe. Who could have predicted this? To lead in the 21st Century, Nouwen suggests learning to lead like Jesus. He outlines three temptations (taken from the temptation of Christ in the wilderness) of a leader and the three spiritual disciplines (based on Jesus' words with Peter in John 21) that will allow that leader to overcome these temptations and walk with God. Commit as a team to practice one of these disciplines together and after a month, share your experiences with one another.

---

24. Henri Nouwen, In the Name of Jesus, (New York: Crossroad Publishers, 1991), 3-4. The chart is a summary of the book. You might want to get copies for each team member in order to fully understand Nouwen's message and to implement the recommended practices. Chart quotations from pages 31, 50, and 69-70 respectively.

From Relevance to Prayer	From Popularity to Ministry	From Leading to Being Led
Temptation One: To Be Relevant	Temptation Two: To Be Spectacular	Temptation Three: To Be Powerful
The Question: "Do You Love Me?"	The Task: "Feed My Sheep"	The Challenge: "Somebody Else Will Take You"
The Discipline: Contemplative Prayer	The Discipline: Confession and Forgiveness	The Discipline: Theological Reflection
"Christian leaders cannot simply be persons who have well-informed opinions about the burning issues of our time. Their leadership must be rooted in the permanent, intimate relationship with Jesus, and they need to find there the source for their words, advice, and guidance. Through the discipline of contemplative prayer, Christian leaders have to learn to listen again and again to the voice of love and to find there the wisdom and courage to address whatever issue presents itself to them."	"Ministers and priests are also called to be full members of their communities, are accountable to them and need their affection and support, and are called to minister with their whole being, including their wounded selves … They need a place where they can share their deep pain and struggles with people who do not need them, but who can guide them ever deeper into the mystery of God's love."	Seminaries and Divinity Schools must become places "where people are trained in true discernment of the signs of the time. This cannot be just an intellectual training. It requires a deep spiritual formation involving the whole person—body, mind, and heart. I think we are only half aware of how secular even theological schools have become. Formation in the mind of Christ, who did not cling to power but emptied himself, taking the form of a slave, is not what most seminaries are about."

TEAM NOTES

Ideas for more meaningful SERVICE together as a team.

CONCLUSION

The expectation for a workbook like this is not that any individual or team would read straight through, implementing every exercise. Instead, our hope is that what is useful would be used and what is not would be ignored. Therefore, a conclusion seems quite silly. This is especially true when we realize that the pursuit of team health is never fully accomplished. Therefore, the reader would do well to remember that there are endless exercises that could be employed to help strengthen a team in the 25 areas at which we have looked. You know your team better than anyone, and it is our prayer that this little book of exercises would merely stir within you a little creativity with which to plan activities that would benefit the health of your team. Remember that team life, in general, and team meetings, specifically, are not all about business and production, but are wholly about God's work in and through the team. We will leave you with one more quotation upon which to reflect, and may it serve as a mission statement of sorts for any team that God privileges you with participation in:

Our priority mission is intimacy with God, and our secondary mission is intimacy and authenticity in community with the family of God. Our outcome mission is vitality in well-managed service to others. If and when we finally figure this out, we will indeed be on the road to Becoming a Healthy Team.[25]

---

25. Macchia, 24.

ABOUT THE AUTHORS

Stephen A. Macchia, M.Div., D.Min. is Founder and President of Leadership Transformations and Director of the Pierce Center for Disciple-Building at Gordon-Conwell Theological Seminary. He is the author of several books, including *Becoming A Healthy Church* (Baker Books) and *Crafting A Rule of Life* (InterVarsity Press). He and his wife Ruth are proud parents of two grown children, Nathan and Rebekah.

For more information, please visit:
www.LeadershipTransformations.org
www.HealthyChurch.net
www.RuleOfLife.com

Justin Schell, MAR, MAME, has been a part of or led teams on 4 continents, including his current work as Director of Executive Projects for the Lausanne Movement. He is a regular instructor for the Perspectives on the World Christian Movement Course, consults with churches around the U.S. on strategic mission engagement for the local church, and provides personal coaching and spiritual direction for emerging leaders. He also facilitates a city-wide mission network in Tulsa, Oklahoma which has the vision of 'Tulsa Believers Partnering to Reach 100 Unreached People Groups through God's Power by 2040.' He lives in Tulsa with his favorite team: his wife Megan and his children Henry and Evie.

OTHER BOOKS BY STEPHEN A. MACCHIA

Wellspring: 31-Days to Whole-Hearted Living the Bible is filled with more than 50 different depictions of the heart, such as hardened, humble, deceitful and grateful. God's desire is to woo his followers to devote their whole heart to him in all aspects of their personal life and worship: loving God with "all" their heart...as well as with their soul, mind, and strength.

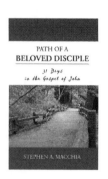

Path of a Beloved Disciple: 31-Days in the Gospel of John Welcome to the delightful journey of discipleship! Jesus invites us to say an enthusiastic "Yes!" to his beckoning call: Come close, draw near, and follow me. This is exactly what John the Beloved Disciple said long ago and it's our invitation to intimacy today. Becoming a "beloved disciple" of Jesus is the focus of the 31 reflections contained in this devotional guide. Each reading covers one of the 10 traits of a healthy disciple (taken from *Becoming a Healthy Disciple*) or one of the 21 chapters of the Gospel of John which feature different portraits of Christ.

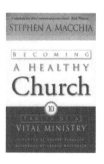

In **Becoming a Healthy Church**, Stephen A. Macchia illustrates how to move beyond church growth to church health. Healthy growth is a process that requires risk taking, lifestyle changes, and ongoing evaluation. This book is a practical, hands-on manual to launch you and your church into a process of positive change. Available in 4 Languages: English, Chinese, Korean, Spanish.

Becoming a Healthy Disciple explores the ten traits of a healthy disciple, including a vital prayer life, evangelistic outreach, worship, servanthood, and stewardship. He applies to individual Christians the ten characteristics of a healthy church outlined in his previous book, *Becoming a Healthy Church*. Discipleship is a lifelong apprenticeship to Jesus Christ, the master teacher. Macchia looks to John the beloved disciple as an example of a life lived close to Christ.

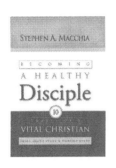

Becoming a Healthy Disciple Small Group Study & Worship Guide is a companion to Steve Macchia's book, *Becoming a Healthy Disciple*. This small group guide provides discussion and worship outlines to enrich your study of the ten traits of a healthy disciple. This 12-week small group resource provides Study, Worship, and Prayer guidelines for each session.

Becoming a Healthy Team is essential for building the kingdom. Stephen A. Macchia offers tried and tested principles and practices to help your leadership team do the same. He'll show you how to Trust, Empower, Assimilate, Manage, and Serve. That spells TEAMS and ultimately success. Filled with scriptural guideposts, *Becoming a Healthy Team* provides practical answers and pointed questions to keep your team on track and moving ahead.

In **Crafting a Rule of Life** Stephen A. Macchia looks to St. Benedict as a guide for discovering your own rule of life in community. It is a process that takes time and concerted effort; you must listen to God and discern what he wants you to be and do for his glory. But through the basic disciplines of Scripture, prayer and reflection in a small group context this practical workbook will lead you forward in a journey toward Christlikeness.

Additional Resources @
SPIRITUALFORMATIONSTORE.COM

Guide to Prayer for All Who Walk With God

The latest from Rueben Job, A Guide to Prayer for All Who Walk With God offers a simple pattern of daily prayer built around weekly themes and organized by the Christian church year. Each week features readings for reflection from such well-known spiritual writers as Francis of Assisi, Teresa of Avila, Dietrich Bonhoeffer, Henri J. M. Nouwen, Sue Monk Kidd, Martin Luther, Julian of Norwich, M. Basil Pennington, Evelyn Underhill, Douglas Steere, and many others.

Guide to Prayer for All Who Seek God

For nearly 20 years, people have turned to the Guide to Prayer series for a daily rhythm of devotion and personal worship. Thousands of readers appreciate the series' simple structure of daily worship, rich spiritual writings, lectionary guidelines, and poignant prayers. Like its predecessors, A Guide to Prayer for All Who Seek God will become a treasured favorite for those hungering for God as the Christian year unfolds.

Guide to Prayer for Ministers and Other Servants

A best-seller for more than a decade! This classic devotional and prayer book includes thematically arranged material for each week of the year as well as themes and schedules for 12 personal retreats. The authors have adopted the following daily format for this prayer book: daily invocations, readings, scripture, reflection, prayers, weekly hymns, benedictions, and printed psalms.

Guide to Prayer for All God's People

A compilation of scripture, prayers and spiritual readings, this inexhaustible resource contains thematically arranged material for each week of the year and for monthly personal retreats. Its contents have made it a sought-after desk reference, a valuable library resource and a cherished companion.

LEADERSHIP
TRANSFORMATIONS INC.

FORMATION | DISCERNMENT | RENEWAL

- Soul Care Retreats and Soul Sabbaths
- Emmaus: Spiritual Leadership Communities
- Selah: Certificate Program in Spiritual Direction (East and West)
- Spiritual Formation Groups
- Spiritual Health Assessments
- Spiritual Discernment for Teams
- Sabbatical Planning
- Spiritual Formation Resources

Visit www.LeadershipTransformations.org
or call (877) TEAM LTI.

18765803R00036

Made in the USA
Middletown, DE
22 March 2015